EXPLORER TRAVEL GUIDES

MOUNTAINS

Chris Oxlade

Raintree is an imprint of Capstone Global Library Limited, a company incorporated in England and Wales having its registered office at 7 Pilgrim Street, London, EC4V 6LB – Registered company number: 6695582

To contact Raintree, please phone 0845 6044371, fax + 44 (0) 1865 312263, or email myorders@raintreepublishers.co.uk.

Text © Capstone Global Library Limited 2014
First published in hardback in 2014
The moral rights of the proprietor have been asserted.

Edited by Adam Miller, Laura Knowles, and Claire Throp
Designed by Steve Mead
Original illustrations © Capstone Global Library Ltd 2014
Illustrated by H L Studios
Picture research by Tracy Cummins
Production by Victoria Fitzgerald
Originated by Capstone Global Library Ltd
Printed in China by China Translation and Printing Services

ISBN 978 1 406 26012 0
17 16 15 14 13
10 9 8 7 6 5 4 3 2 1

British Library Cataloguing in Publication Data
Oxlade, Chris
Mountains. – (Explorer travel guides)
910.9'143-dc23
A full catalogue record for this book is available from the British Library.

Acknowledgements
We would like to thank the following for permission to reproduce photographs: Alamy p. 31 (© Max Stuart); Corbis p. 28 (© HO/Reuters); Getty Images pp. 8 (Jonathan P. Ellgen), 14 (Stephen Collector), 23 (Andrea Solero/AFP), 26 (John Terence Turner), 36 (Eddie Kosmicki/Bloomberg), 37 (Shaun Curry/AFP); Hugh Tuffen p. 12 (© Hugh Tuffen); Neil Champion pp. 5 middle, 34 (© Neil Champion); Shutterstock pp. 4 (© Microstock Man), 5 bottom, 33 (© My Good Images), 5 top, 10 (© Peter Wey), 6 (© cozyta), 15 (© Isabella Pfenninger), 16 (© Lutsan Pavlo), 17 (© Dennis Donohue), 19 (© Narongsak N.), 20, 38 (© Petunyia), 21 (© Lee Prince), 22 (© Martin Lehmann), 39 (© Galyna Andrushko); Superstock pp. 18 (© Wolfgang Kaehler), 25 (© Prisma), 27 (© Henry Georgi/All Canada Photos), 32 (© William Stevenson).

Design elements: Shutterstock (© pchais), (© Nik Merkulov), (© vovan), (© SmileStudio), (© Petrov Stanislav Eduardovich), (© Nataliia Natykach), (© Phecsone).

Cover photograph of Cerro Torre seen from Agostini camp, Los Glaciares National Park, Patagonian Andes, Argentina reproduced with permission of Getty Images (Colin Monteath/Hedgehog House).

We would like to thank Daniel Block for his invaluable help in the preparation of this book.

Every effort has been made to contact copyright holders of material reproduced in this book. Any omissions will be rectified in subsequent printings if notice is given to the publisher.

Disclaimer
All the internet addresses (URLs) given in this book were valid at the time of going to press. However, due to the dynamic nature of the internet, some addresses may have changed, or sites may have changed or ceased to exist since publication. While the author and publisher regret any inconvenience this may cause readers, no responsibility for any such changes can be accepted by either the author or the publisher.

CONTENTS

Some words are shown in bold, **like this**. You can find out what they mean by looking in the glossary.

Don't forget

These boxes will give you handy tips and remind you what to take on your mountain adventures.

Amazing facts

Check out these boxes for amazing mountain facts and figures.

Who's who

Find out more about mountain experts and explorers of the past.

Conservation

Learn about conservation issues relating to mountains.

WELCOME TO THE MOUNTAINS!

You've chosen to explore some of the world's most amazing places! Sights to see in the mountains include towering, rocky, and snow-capped **summits**, vertical cliffs, icy **glaciers**, deep gorges, tumbling streams and rivers, and spectacular views. The mountain peaks themselves are not the only sights. A wide variety of plants and animals live on their slopes. Also, there are the villages and towns of the people who live and work in the mountains.

The great peaks of the Himalayas are the highest of the world's mountain ranges.

What is a mountain?

A mountain is simply a place where the landscape rises steeply above the lower, flatter land around it. There's no rule to say when a hill is high enough to be a mountain. In some countries, a hill about 1,000 metres (3,000 feet) above sea level is thought of as a mountain; in other places, this would just be a small **foothill**.

Most of the world's mountains are part of **mountain ranges**. A mountain range is an area where there are many mountains in a group, or a long line. Enormous mountain ranges include the Himalayas, in Asia; the Andes, in South America; the Rockies, in North America; and the Alps, in Europe. In all, mountains cover about one-quarter of the world's land (not ocean) surface. Many **volcanoes** are also thought of as mountains.

TURN THE PAGE...

Find out about erosion on page 11.

Meet a real-life mountain explorer on pages 34–35.

Learn more about avalanches on page 33.

Amazing facts

The Himalayas contain the highest mountains in the world on land, including the highest of all, Everest at 8,850 metres (29,035 feet). The Andes is the longest range at more than 7,000 kilometres (around 4,500 miles) from north to south.

BEFORE YOU GO

Knowing how mountains are made, what physical features they have, and what the weather is like will help you decide which mountain you would like to visit first.

Mountain types

Mountains are built up in two ways: they are either pushed up by the movement of rocks in Earth's **crust**, or they are built up by volcanic activity. There are three main types of mountains that are built up by the movement of rocks: fold mountains, block mountains, and dome mountains (see diagram, opposite).

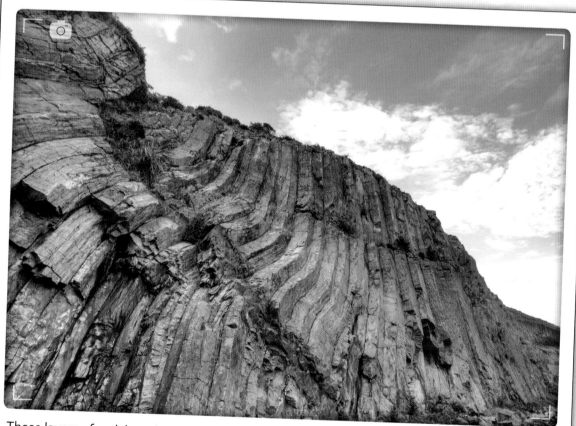

These layers of rock have been folded into mountains by immense forces.

These mountain-building processes take thousands or millions of years. The Himalayas are quite young mountains, but they still began to form more than 600,000 years ago. Since Earth was formed about 4,500 million years ago, many mountain ranges have been built up and worn away. So you've missed the chance to explore them!

Bumping plates

Earth's crust is a solid, rocky skin that covers the planet. It is cracked into many giant pieces, known as **tectonic plates**. The plates move very slowly, and in some places their edges scrunch into each other, or one plate slides under the other. This movement pushes up fold mountains. But sometimes the rocks don't bend to form mountains. Instead, they crack (or fault) and form block mountains.

? Who's who

Alfred Wegener (1880–1930) was a German scientist who realized that the coastlines of South America and Africa fit together like two pieces of a jigsaw. He suggested that Earth's continents are slowly moving, and that about 250 million years ago all the continents were joined together in one giant continent, which he called Pangaea, meaning "all the Earth".

The three types of mountain

Fold mountain	Block mountain	Dome mountain

Rocks scrunch together at edges of tectonic plates

Huge block of rock rises or falls

Molten rock rising from under Earth's crust pushes upwards

Volcanic mountains

A volcano is a place where molten rock (called **magma**) from under Earth's crust makes its way to the surface. The magma solidifies, forming new rock. Over time, the new rock builds up to form a mountain.

Most volcanoes erupt along the edges of tectonic plates, where one plate slides under another. Rock in the lower of the two plates gets very hot and melts, and the magma forces its way to the surface. Volcanoes also form at places called hot spots in Earth's crust, where magma from below pushes upwards. The islands of Hawaii are the tops of volcanoes that have grown over a hot spot on the floor of the Pacific Ocean.

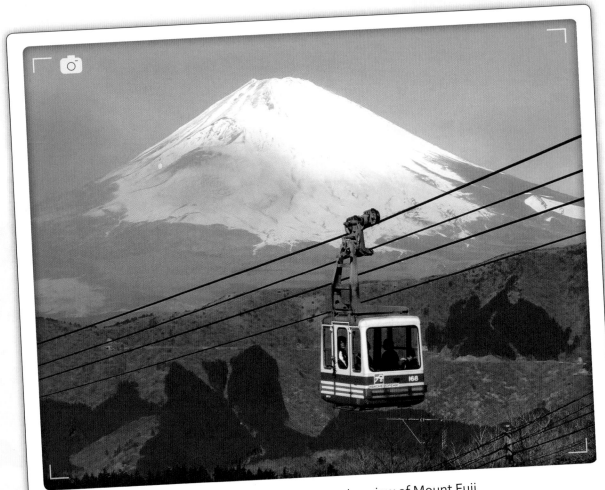

Travelling by cable car allows people to see an amazing view of Mount Fuji in Japan.

Types of volcano

There are several different types of volcano, but the two types that build up the highest mountains are stratovolcanoes and shield volcanoes. Stratovolcanoes erupt **ash** and thick **lava**, which build up into steep-sided, cone-shaped mountains. Shield volcanoes erupt runny lava. This flows down the volcano's slopes and solidifies, building up a mountain with gently sloping sides.

So, which mountains would you like to visit? The high, icy peaks of a fold mountain range or the crater of a fiery volcano?

The two main types of volcano

stratovolcano

shield volcano

🧳 Don't forget

All mountain exploring can be dangerous, but **active volcanoes** have extra hazards! Hazards include red-hot lava, poisonous gases coming from the ground, and **pyroclastic flows**, which are avalanches of roasting-hot ash. You'll need some special kit such as sturdy boots to protect your feet from hot, sharp rocks on volcanoes. If you're going near lava flows, you'll need to borrow a heat-reflecting suit. This is covered with metal foil so that the heat from the lava bounces off.

Mountain climate

The big thing you'll notice about exploring mountains is the weather! The **climate** on mountains is generally colder, wetter, and windier than it is on the plains below the mountains. The atmosphere is colder higher up, because it is not warmed as much by heat from Earth's surface. It's windier because air has to flow up, over, and around mountains, and it gets squeezed as it does, which makes winds stronger. It's wetter because rain clouds form if moist air rises to pass over mountains. The air cools as it rises, and water vapour in it turns to liquid water, which makes clouds and rain. Cold temperatures also mean that snow falls on mountains when it's raining on the plains below.

These jagged peaks have been made as the weather has cracked and broken their rock.

Weathering and erosion

The harsh weather breaks up the rocks that mountains are made of. This process is called weathering. When water freezes in cracks in rock, it can split the rock apart, and particles of rock blown along in strong winds knock pieces off rocks. Other rocks may dissolve or become soft in water. The loose bits of rock fall down the mountainside, are washed away by water, or are blown away. Gradually, mountains are worn away. This process is known as **erosion**.

Amazing facts

Mountain ranges can create deserts. They force air upwards, which makes the air cool, clouds form, and rain fall. By the time the air reaches the far side of the mountains, there is no rain left to fall. The land here is very dry, and the area is known as rain shadow. The Tibetan Plateau is a very dry area in the rain shadow of the Himalayas.

The physical features of mountains

saddle or col
face
summit
ridge
glacier
crevasse

INTERVIEW WITH A VOLCANOLOGIST

Dr Hugh Tuffen is a volcanologist at Lancaster University, UK.

Q: What do you do in your job as a volcanologist?
A: I get to visit both active and **extinct** volcanoes in exciting countries such as Iceland, Chile, and Japan. This is to watch volcanic eruptions and to collect samples of lava and **pumice** formed in past eruptions.

Q: When did you become interested in volcanoes?
A: When I was seven, I got a book about volcanoes and kept on reading it again and again. I loved looking at the pictures of lava rising up from under the ground and making new mountains. I found out that some of the mountains in the UK are actually extinct volcanoes that erupted a long time ago. I started to dream that they were active again and I had to climb them to rescue people who were trapped in the ash!

Q: Is there anything in particular that you enjoy about volcanoes or visiting volcanoes?

A: I love visiting volcanoes because they are exciting, wild places that are formed in dramatic eruptions. I love climbing volcanoes, seeing the spectacular views, thinking about how the earth under our feet is alive, and then bathing in a hot spring!

Q: Have you ever seen a volcano erupting?

A: I have been lucky to see several volcanoes erupting. The most memorable one was Puyehue Cordon-Caulle in Chile. We camped close to the crater as explosions sent a plume of ash high into the sky above us and sent out huge booming noises that kept us awake all night. In the morning, our tents were covered in ash.

Q: Do you have a favourite volcano?

A: My favourite volcano is Torfajökull in Iceland. I've been lucky to spend many months there and have got to know the volcano very well. It last erupted in 1477.

Q: Are there any volcanoes that you would particularly like to visit?

A: I would love to visit Mt Erebus in Antarctica. I'd like to see its boiling lava lake, its deep crater, and the ice caves made by heat from the crater.

Q: What hazard of visiting volcanoes scares you the most?

A: I am most scared of pyroclastic flows. When camping on the side of an active volcano, I always avoid valleys as pyroclastic flows tend to travel down them. It is much safer to stay on higher ground.

DISCOVERING NATURE

Vast numbers of plants and animals live in the world's mountain ranges. The plants and animals are **adapted** to the harsh conditions, and some even survive on the snowy, rocky mountain summits. These distinct communities of plants and animals are known as **biomes**.

Plant zones

Imagine climbing right from the bottom of a mountain to its summit. You might walk through **coniferous** forests on the lower slopes. Then you'll find **alpine** meadows. Eventually, you would reach a height where no plants can grow, known as the summit zone. These different levels of a mountain are known as plant zones. They exist because of the different climate at different levels of a mountain. The main zones are **deciduous**, coniferous, alpine, **tundra**, and summit.

Lush green forests grow on mountain slopes in Peru.

Small plants come into flower when snow melts in spring in alpine meadows.

Plant adaptations

Mountain plants are adapted to life at high **altitude**. For example, alpine flowers can grow where there is very little soil. Their roots grow into cracks in the rocks, allowing them to hang on in strong winds. They also grow low to the ground, to avoid being damaged by the wind.

? Who's who

Joseph Hooker (1817–1911) was a British botanist. He went on many scientific expeditions around the world to study plants. He visited the Himalayas, the Rockies, and the Atlas Mountains in North Africa, discovering many new **species** of plants, and collecting thousands of samples to take back to the Royal Botanic Gardens in Kew, London, where he worked.

Fur coats

Mountain animals have thick coats to insulate their bodies from the cold, and the coats get thicker as winter approaches. The yak, which lives in the Himalayas, has two layers of fur: a dense layer of short hair with long, shaggy fur on top. The snow leopard has fur on the bottom of its paws, and it can wrap its furry tail around itself like a blanket.

Sure-footed ibex search for food on the steep, rocky slopes of the Alps.

Don't forget

Mountain animals are tricky to get close to. Often, they can walk on steep slopes that are hard and dangerous for humans to get to. Smaller animals hide quickly under rocks if you get too close! Make sure you take a pair of binoculars or a small telescope, so you can get a good look at them from a distance. You could also take a guide to animal shapes and footprints to help you identify the animals.

Living at altitude

High in the mountains, the air is thinner than it is lower down. This means there is less oxygen for animals to breathe. Llamas live high in the Andes. They have large lungs, and also have more red blood cells in their blood than any other mammal. Lungs transfer oxygen from the air into red blood cells, and the cells carry it to where it's needed in the body.

Surviving winter

In winter, it's hard for animals to find food in the mountains. Some animals move to lower altitudes, where the weather is less harsh. Other animals **hibernate** instead. For example, the marmot, which lives on mountains throughout Europe, Asia, and western North America, hibernates for about six months in a burrow under the alpine meadows where it lives.

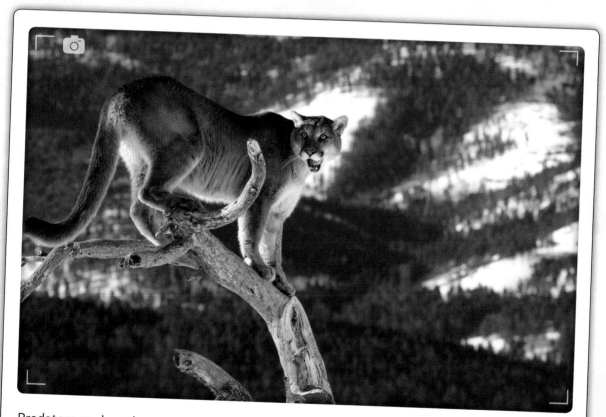

Predators, such as the mountain lion, hunt over a large area because food is scarce. Only a few mountain lions could survive in a range of 78 square kilometres (30 square miles).

MOUNTAIN LIFE

Rocks, snow and ice, plants, and wildlife are not the only things you'll see when you explore mountains. You'll also meet the people who have made the mountains their home because there are good pastures for animals, space to live, and beautiful surroundings. Farmers living on the slopes of volcanoes grow crops in the rich volcanic soil.

Adapting to the mountains

Reasons for living in mountains differ between poorer and wealthier nations. Many tribes of people have lived in the mountains for hundreds and even thousands of years. Over time, they have learned the skills needed to survive, such as how to keep warm and grow crops. Like mountain animals, people who live at high altitudes have become adapted to the thin air.

The **indigenous** people of Ecuador have more red blood cells to carry oxygen around their bodies than average humans.

Machu Picchu

The spectacular mountain settlement of Machu Picchu in Peru was built about 550 years ago by the Inca people. The Incas built here because the mountains were a natural protection against invaders. People who live in the mountains around Machu Picchu today live in a similar way to the Incas, growing crops and raising animals.

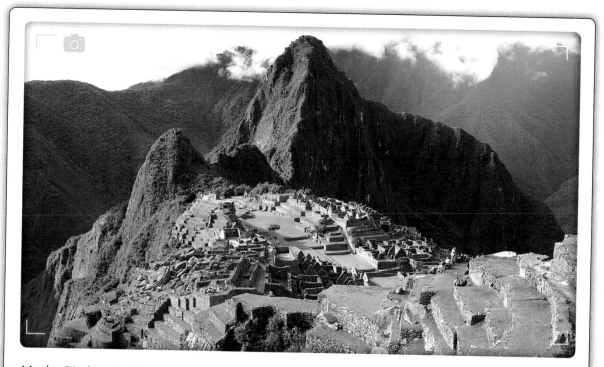

Machu Picchu stands 2,430 metres (7,972 feet) up in the Andes.

Conservation

In some mountain areas, such as the country of Nepal, people have cut down forests, mainly for firewood. Nepal lost a quarter of its forest between 1990 and 2010 alone. With the trees gone, the soil is washed away, and floods and landslides are more common. Today, people are trying to prevent illegal **deforestation**, and to introduce alternatives to wood for fuel, such as solar power. In many areas, mountain forests are now managed by governments to balance use, conservation, and recreation.

Working in the mountains

Most of the people who live in the remote mountain areas of Asia and South America are small-scale farmers or herders. They grow crops for themselves, to barter or to sell at local markets, or keep animals such as llamas and yaks, which they trade. Some people live as **nomads**, moving from place to place to find new pastures for their animals.

Animal helpers

Herd animals are important for mountain people. In the Andes, people have kept llamas for thousands of years as **pack animals**, for carrying goods. People use the llamas' wool to make clothing, rugs, and even ropes, their hides to make clothes, their dung as fuel for fires, and eat their meat. In the Himalayas and Tibetan Plateau, people keep yaks, which are large animals like cows. The yaks provide milk, butter, and meat, are used as pack animals, and even for yak racing!

Farmers build terraces on steep mountain slopes to create flat fields for growing crops.

Growing crops

When you visit many mountainous areas of the world, you'll see long, narrow fields on mountain sides. These are called terraces. They make space for farmers to grow crops such as rice, corn, and potatoes on steep slopes. They also help to stop soil being washed away in heavy rain.

Conservation

The world's mountains are important resources for forestry and energy, and leisure. But in many places, local people are ignored by the mining, forestry, and energy industries that take the resources. In the past, people have even been forced from their land, but today, many mountain areas are protected, and local people control which industries are allowed to operate.

Copper ore is dug out at the Bingham Canyon Mine in the mountains of Utah, USA. The mine is one of the biggest human-made holes in the world!

Early explorations

Every good explorer should know about the adventurous people who first set out into the mountains. The world's mountain ranges are like barriers to travel. Thousands of years ago, people faced long and treacherous journeys if they wanted to cross mountains to find new places to live, or to trade goods. There were no roads, maps, or modern clothing. In ancient times, armies sometimes lost thousands of troops to the cold as they crossed mountain ranges to explore and conquer other countries.

Today, you can take road or rail tunnels under some mountain ranges, such as the Alps, but in most places you still have to go over mountain **passes** to get from one side to the other.

Roads and railways have opened the way for everyone to travel in the mountains.

Scaling the peaks

In the 19th century, explorers started to climb mountains just for the challenge of getting to the top. They started in the Alps, climbing peaks such as Mont Blanc and the Eiger. Today, mountaineers climb in all the world's mountain ranges. In 1953, Tenzing Norgay and Edmund Hillary became the first climbers to reach the summit of the world's highest mountain, Mount Everest.

This body was found preserved in ice high in the Alps. It is 5,300 years old, and shows that people crossed over mountains in the distant past.

Who's who

Reinhold Messner (born 1944) is an Italian mountain climber who achieved many mountaineering firsts. In 1978, he became one of the first two people to climb Mount Everest without using oxygen to breathe. In 1980, he climbed Everest again, but this time solo. Later, he became the first mountaineer to reach the top of all 14 mountains in the world that are taller than 8,000 metres (26,247 feet).

PLANNING YOUR TRIP

There are lots of things to decide before you set off to explore the mountains. Firstly, you'll need to choose which mountains to visit. Read some guide books and study some maps to help you decide. Now you can decide when to go, how to travel, what equipment to bring, and who to take with you.

When to go

When you travel to the mountains depends on what sort of exploring and what kind of activities you want to do. Travelling around in the mountains is easier in summer, when snow and ice melt away, and mountain passes are open. But you'll need to go in winter if you want to do winter sports, such as skiing. You might want to visit an active volcano. The best places to go include the Big Island of Hawaii, or Stromboli, in Italy, where volcanoes erupt nearly all the time.

Conservation

Exploring mountains can often cause environmental problems. Try to be responsible as you explore. For example, never leave any rubbish behind, stay on paths and trails to reduce erosion, don't camp in one place for more than a few days, and don't cut wood for fuel. You should also follow local customs so that you don't upset local people.

Amazing facts

When Mount St Helens volcano in Washington State, USA, began to erupt in 1980, thousands of people flocked to the area because they wanted to see an eruption for themselves. Many visitors ignored police road blocks to get close to the action. They thought they were still a safe distance away, but there was a giant explosion and a pyroclastic flow swept over the landscape. Fifty-seven people were killed when they were buried by the hot ash.

In summer, you can travel over high mountain passes on local buses.

What to wear

Mountain clothes must keep out rain, wind, and cold. That means wearing a base layer for warmth and to take sweat away from your skin, a middle layer for warmth, and a waterproof outer layer. When it's warm and wet, you need a "breathable" outer layer of clothes, which keeps out rain, but that lets sweat escape.

You need strong boots, with good grip, for walking on steep, rocky ground. For snow and ice, you'll need crampons on your boots, which have metal spikes underneath. Trekking poles, like thin walking sticks, will help you climb steep mountain slopes.

snow goggles

ice axe

waterproof jacket

waterproof trousers

stiff boots

crampons

It's important to think about warmth and safety when dressing for mountain climbing.

More equipment

For long trips, you may need a tent or other form of shelter, a sleeping bag, a cooking stove, and other camping equipment. But make sure it's lightweight, because you'll have to carry it in a rucksack. You'll also need to bring water, or a way to make the water you find along the way safe to drink. Take some equipment for navigation, including maps, a compass, and a **GPS receiver**.

You'll also need an expert to show you the way, and to teach you how to use climbing equipment such as ropes and harnesses, and possibly a few tanks of oxygen if there's a danger of **altitude sickness**.

Don't forget

Snow reflects sunlight very well, and if you look at it for too long, your eyes could be damaged, making them swell. This is known as snow blindness. So you'll need snow goggles to protect them. You might also need bottles of oxygen, which help you breathe, and stop you getting altitude sickness (see page 30).

Cross-country skis are great for moving fast across snowy landscapes.

EXPLORER TRAVEL GUIDES

WHO'S GOING WITH YOU?

Imagine you're going on an expedition to the mountains. Who would you take as your travelling companions? Here are some ideas.

Expedition member: Tenzing Norgay (1914–1986)

Tenzing Norgay (on the right) was a Tibetan mountaineer who was the first person to reach the top of Mount Everest, along with New Zealand's Edmund Hillary. Tenzing started working on mountain expeditions as a porter, carrying equipment for other climbers. Climbing Everest made him world famous.

Potential job: Mountain guide

Expedition member: Kenton Cool (born 1973)

Kenton Cool is a British mountaineer. He has reached the summit of Everest an amazing 10 times, and the summits of many more of the world's tallest mountains. He has even skied down Cho Oyu, the world's sixth-highest mountain! He is also one of the best mountain guides in the world.

Potential job: Expedition manager

Expedition member: Volcanologist

A volcanologist is a type of geologist who specializes in volcanoes. He or she could tell you about the features of the volcanoes you visit, such as craters and lava flows, and keep you safe on a volcano.

Potential job: Volcano guide

Expedition member: Geography teacher

Your geography teacher should know all about mountains! He or she will be able to tell you all about how mountains are made, and point out all the different parts of mountains you'll see, and about mountain people and the way they live.

Potential job: Expedition teacher

Expedition member: Wildlife expert

A wildlife expert could show you interesting plants and animals during your expeditions, and tell you all about them (what they eat, how they live, and how they are adapted to mountains).

Potential job: Mountain wildlife expert

MOUNTAIN SURVIVAL

The hazards you'll encounter when exploring mountain tops include severe weather, steep ground, slippery snow and ice, **avalanches**, and lightning. You need to protect yourself against hypothermia (getting extremely cold), frostbite, and dangerous falls. Never set out if the weather forecast is bad.

Amazing facts

During a thunderstorm, a summit is a dangerous place to be. Mountaineers have been killed by lightning in the past. Mountain storms can form quickly and there is often nowhere to shelter. Climbers and hikers are encouraged to climb during the morning because there is far less chance of a storm coming before midday.

Altitude sickness

The higher you go on a mountain, the thinner the air gets, so there is less oxygen to breathe. At an altitude of about 3,000 metres (about 10,000 feet) or more, you start to notice that it gets harder to breathe. Many people begin to feel sick, have headaches, and feel weak. This is called acute mountain sickness or altitude sickness. This can go away after a day, but you might have to go back down the mountain to recover.

If something goes wrong...

Sometimes, no matter how careful people are, things go wrong in the mountains. People get injured, or fall ill, or get stuck on cliffs, or get lost in bad weather. You can try to attract help with a flashing torch or by blowing a whistle, or call a mountain rescue team by phone.

Don't forget

An emergency shelter will protect you from the wind and rain if you get stuck on a mountain. You could take a large waterproof bag to climb into, a small tent, or a group shelter, like a tent without poles, that three or four people can fit inside.

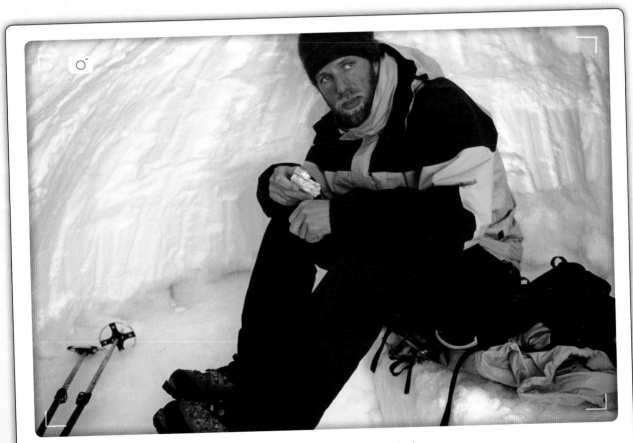

This mountaineer has dug a snow cave to use as a temporary shelter.

Crossing crevasses

A crevasse is a giant crack in a glacier, which can be more than 30 metres (about 100 feet) deep. Never cross a glacier without an expert guide to show you a safe route, as crevasses can be hidden under thin layers of snow. Getting out of a crevasse is normally impossible without help, and equipment such as harnesses and ropes.

These mountaineers are looking for a safe place to cross a glacier in the Karakoram mountains of Pakistan.

 ## Amazing facts

Avalanches move frighteningly fast. An avalanche of powdery snow falling down a steep slope travels at speeds of up to 250 kilometres (155 miles) per hour – as fast as a high-speed train. So there's no way of outrunning an avalanche.

Avalanches

An avalanche is a slide of snow down the side of a mountain. Avalanches are very dangerous to mountain explorers and **off-piste** skiers. They can sweep you downhill and then bury you under heavy snow. To avoid avalanches, read avalanche warnings and stay clear of mountain slopes where avalanches could strike. If you are unlucky enough to be caught in an avalanche, try swimming upwards through the snow before it stops. If you get buried, try to make a space to breathe.

Don't forget

If there is a risk of avalanches where you are planning to go, you should take a radio locator beacon with you. Then rescuers will be able to find you more quickly if you are buried. You could also carry an avalanche airbag. This will blow up like a balloon if you are tumbled over by an avalanche, and help to stop you being buried.

Avalanches start when deep snow on a steep slope becomes unstable.

INTERVIEW WITH A MOUNTAIN EXPLORER

Neil Champion is a mountaineering and climbing instructor in the United Kingdom.

Q: When did you start exploring mountains?
A: I joined the Outdoor Pursuits club at my secondary school when I was 13. Each year, we went to North Wales for a week at Easter, where I was introduced to abseiling, climbing, hill walking, and wild camping. Great stuff!

Q: What do you like about exploring mountains?
A: Getting away from the crowds, being self-reliant, and the sheer fun and physical nature of mountaineering all attract me, as well as the wonderful landscapes you pass through.

Q: Do you have a favourite mountain?
A: I think the Cuillin of Skye, in Scotland, are my favourite. I have walked and climbed in them on a dozen or more different occasions and I still can't pretend to know them. They combine challenge, a fantastic landscape, and remoteness, all to the right degree.

Q: Is there a particular mountain you would like to climb?

A: Island Peak (almost 6,200 metres (20,300 feet) high) in Nepal. It's the mountain Edmund Hillary and Tenzing Norgay climbed in 1953 before they went on to conquer Everest. I'd like to succeed with that one.

Q: Do you have any mountaineering heroes?

A: Bill Tilman and Eric Shipton, two mountaineers who wandered in the Himalayas around 80 years ago and wrote some great accounts of their adventures.

Q: Have you ever got lost in the mountains?

A: Yes, lots of times! The important thing is not to panic and make a plan to relocate yourself using your map, compass, and memory of the ground you have just walked over.

Q: Is there anything that scares you about mountains?

A: Avalanches scare me. They don't respect age or climbing ability, and in spite of lots of scientific research into what causes them, they remain unpredictable. I almost got caught in one when ice climbing in the Alps. It frightened the life out of me!

Q: What's your favourite piece of clothing or equipment?

A: I think it has to be a head band. I use them all the time in the hills. They don't make your head boil like a woolly hat can, but they keep your ears warm. I think the head band is an unsung hero.

CONSERVATION

Many of the world's mountain environments are threatened by human activities, even in the most remote places, where almost nobody lives. Our activities, such as mining and building dams, are affecting the animals, plants, and people that live on mountains, the people who live in mountains, and the landscape of the mountains themselves.

Tourism and leisure

More and more people are visiting and exploring mountains to enjoy their beauty, walk up them, climb on them, and for winter sports such as skiing and snowboarding. These people may leave pollution, erode the landscape, and use up precious resources such as water. The development of tourist facilities, such as ski resorts, can bring jobs and income to local people.

As skiing becomes more popular, new ski resorts are built in the mountains.

Effects of global warming

Global warming is the gradual warming of the air in Earth's atmosphere, which most scientists agree is caused by activities such as burning fossil fuels and cutting down rainforests. In the mountains, the main effect of global warming is that glaciers are shrinking. In summer, melting glaciers are an important source of water for mountain animals, people, and crops. Water could be in short supply if glaciers melt completely.

Conservation

Building dams on mountain rivers means that valleys are flooded, along with the villages in them, and water supplies are often lost. Local people are often powerless to stop these developments. But they can protest against them, and sometimes they win the battle.

In 2012, villagers in the Lahaul Valley in northern India protested against the building of several large dams that would affect 26 villages.

The importance of mountains

Most people in the world don't live on mountains, or even near mountains. They might not care about what happens to mountains, as long as they get the things they need from them, such as water, raw materials, and energy. But mountains are very important to the plants, animals, and people who live there, and to the people who love to visit and explore them.

We need to look after mountains in the same way that we need to look after other parts of the world, such as rainforests and oceans. Damaging the mountains through mining, cutting down trees, building too many dams, and overusing the mountains for leisure will harm them and affect the lives of mountain people.

People find it rewarding to climb a mountain and to enjoy the view.

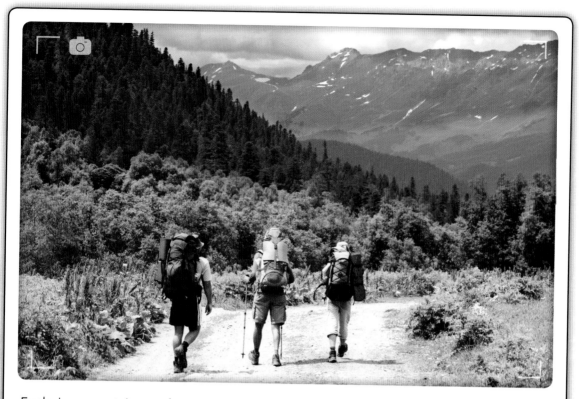

Exploring mountains can be an exciting and enjoyable experience.

Why visit the mountains?

Mountains are spectacular, awe-inspiring places to visit and explore. There are wild, remote, and beautiful places where people can escape to from their busy, everyday lives, perhaps catch a glimpse of a rare mountain animal, get to know how local people live and work, and do some exciting sports. There are still many mountains that nobody has visited, and some summits that nobody has climbed. So plan a trip, find some companions, get equipped, and get out and explore the mountains!

Don't forget

Take a camera to photograph the places you explore, the things you see, and the people you meet. There's a saying about exploring the world's wild places: "Take only photographs, leave only footprints." So take as many photographs as you like, but take away your rubbish, and leave everything exactly as you found it.

WORLD MOUNTAIN RANGES

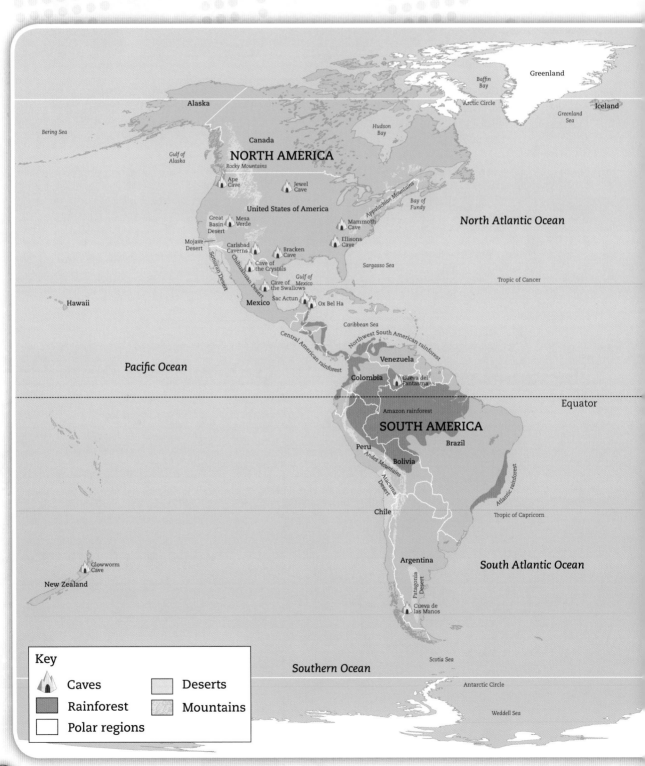

Greenland

Baffin
Bay

Alaska

Arctic Circle

Iceland

Greenland
Sea

Bering Sea

Hudson
Bay

Gulf of
Alaska

Canada

NORTH AMERICA

Rocky Mountains

North Atlantic Ocean

Ape
Cave

Jewel
Cave

Appalachian Mountains

Bay of
Fundy

United States of America

Great
Basin
Desert

Mesa
Verde

Mammoth
Cave

Mojave
Desert

Carlsbad
Caverns

Bracken
Cave

Ellisons
Cave

Sargasso Sea

Cave of
the Crystals

Tropic of Cancer

Chihuahuan Desert

Gulf of
Mexico

Sonoran Desert

Cave of
the Swallows

Hawaii

Mexico

Sac Actun

Ox Bel Ha

Caribbean Sea

Central American rainforest

Northwest South American rainforest

Venezuela

Pacific Ocean

Colombia

Cueva del
Fantasma

Equator

Amazon rainforest

SOUTH AMERICA

Peru

Brazil

Andes Mountains

Bolivia

Atacama
Desert

Atlantic rainforest

Chile

Tropic of Capricorn

Glowworm
Cave

Argentina

South Atlantic Ocean

New Zealand

Patagonia
Desert

Cueva de
las Manos

Scotia Sea

Southern Ocean

Antarctic Circle

Weddell Sea

Key

🔺 Caves

Deserts

Rainforest

Mountains

Polar regions

This map shows you where to find some of the world's mountains. There are many other exciting places to discover. Why not explore the oceans, caves, deserts, and rainforests shown on the map?

Arctic Ocean

Barents Sea

Kara Sea

Laptev Sea

East Siberian Sea

Norwegian Sea

Sweden

Finland

Arctic Circle

Bering Sea

Norway

Ural Mountains

Russia

North Sea

Sea of Okhotsk

Fingal's Cave

United Kingdom

Gaping Gill

Dan-yr-Ogof

EUROPE

Eisriesenwelt

Postojna Cave

Krubera-Voronja

Bay of Biscay

France

Chauvet Cave

Alps

Austria

Slovenia

Lascaux Caves

Raymonden Shelter

Black Sea

Georgia

Caucasus Mountains

Azykh Cave

Caspian Sea

Kara Kum Desert

Karakoram Range

Takla Makan Desert

Gobi Desert

Sea of Japan

Japan

Atlas Mountains

Mediterranean Sea

ASIA

China

Yellow Sea

Pacific Ocean

Himalayas

Sahara Desert

Red Sea

Arabian Desert

Thar Desert

Bhimbetka

India

East China Sea

AFRICA

Arabian Sea

Bay of Bengal

Southeast Asian rainforest

South China Sea

Malaysia

Sulu Sea

Sarawak Chamber

Central African rainforest

Banda Sea

Indonesian rainforest

Indonesia

Indian Ocean

AUSTRALASIA

Coral Sea

Mozambique Channel

Madagascar

Madagascan rainforest

Great Sandy Desert

Simpson Desert

Australia

Gibson Desert

Namib Desert

Botswana

Kalahari Desert

Great Victoria Desert

Northern Australian rainforest

South Africa

Drakensberg Mountains

Great Dividing Range

Blombos Cave

Tasman Sea

N

Southern Ocean

Antarctic Circle

ANTARCTICA

Mount Erebus

Ross Sea

FACT FILE

THE HIGHEST MOUNTAINS

Mountain	Range	Height in metres (feet)
Everest	Himalayas	8,850 metres (29,035 feet)
K2	Karakoram	8,611 metres (28,251 feet)
Kangchenjunga	Himalayas	8,586 metres (28,169 feet)
Lhotse	Himalayas	8,501 metres (27,890 feet)
Makalu	Himalayas	8,463 metres (27,766 feet)
Cho Oyu	Himalayas	8,201 metres (26,906 feet)
Dhaulagiri	Himalayas	8,167 metres (26,795 feet)
Manaslu	Himalayas	8,163 metres (26,781 feet)
Nanga Parbat	Himalayas	8,126 metres (26,660 feet)
Annapurna	Himalayas	8,091 metres (26,545 feet)

THE HIGHEST MOUNTAINS BY CONTINENT

Continent	Mountain	Height in metres (feet)
Asia	Everest	8,850 metres (29,035 feet)
South America	Aconcagua	6,959 metres (22,831 feet)
North America	McKinley	6,194 metres (20,322 feet)
Africa	Kilimanjaro	5,895 metres (19,341 feet)
Europe	Elbrus	5,642 metres (18,510 feet)
Antarctica	Vinson Massif	4,892 metres (16,050 feet)
Australasia	Kosciusko	2,228 metres (7,310 feet)

THE LONGEST MOUNTAIN RANGES

Range	Continent	Length in kilometres (miles)
The Andes	South America	7,242 kilometres (4,500 miles)
The Rockies	North America	6,035 kilometres (3,750 miles)
The Himalayas (including the Karakoram and Hindu Kush)	Asia	3,862 kilometres (2,400 miles)
The Great Dividing Range	Australia	3,621 kilometres (2,250 miles)
The Trans-Antarctic	Antarctica	3,541 kilometres (2,200 miles)

Historic first ascents

These are the people who were first to the top of some of the world's most famous mountains.

Mountain	Range	Climbers
Mont Blanc	Alps	Michel-Gabriel Paccard and his porter, Jacques Balmat (Sardinia) 1786
Eiger	Alps	Charles Barrington and guides (UK, Switzerland) 1858
Matterhorn	Alps	Edward Whymper (UK) and others 1865
McKinley	Alaska Range	Hudson Stuck and others (United States) 1913
Annapurna	Himalayas	Maurice Herzog and Louis Lachenal (France) 1950
Everest	Himalayas	Tenzing Norgay (Nepal) and Edmund Hillary (New Zealand) 1953
K2	Karakoram	Achille Compagnoni and Lino Lacedelli (Italy) 1954

Underwater mountains

- Mountains under the oceans (called seamounts) dwarf the mountains on dry land! They form where magma leaks out from under Earth's crust onto the ocean floor, so they are really underwater volcanoes.
- The highest seamount is Mauna Loa, at 10,200 metres (33,465 feet). Its top forms part of the island of Hawaii.
- The longest mountain range is the mid-ocean ridge, which stretches about 65,000 kilometres (40,000 miles) around Earth, under the Atlantic and Pacific Oceans.

GLOSSARY

active volcano volcano that is erupting, or which has recently erupted and may erupt again soon

adapted describes a plant or animal that has features that allow it to live in its habitat

alpine to do with high mountains

altitude how high above the level of the sea something is

altitude sickness medical problem that happens because of the lack of oxygen at very high altitudes. People need oxygen to breathe.

ash tiny particles of rock formed when magma is blasted into tiny pieces as it leaves a volcano, cools, and becomes solid

avalanche slide of snow down the side of a mountain

biome community of plants and animals that live in a very large habitat, such as a mountain range

climate pattern of weather that happens in a place over a long time

coniferous tree with leaves like needles that do not fall off in autumn, and that grows cones

crevasse deep crack in a glacier

crust solid, rocky skin of Earth that makes up the surface we stand on

deciduous describes a tree that loses its leaves in autumn and gets new leaves in spring

deforestation cutting down the trees in a forest, leaving bare ground where trees can't grow again

erosion process that wears away rocks and breaks down mountains

extinct describes a volcano that is dead – it will never erupt again

face sloping side of a mountain

foothill hill between a high mountain range and the plains below

glacier slow-moving river of ice that flows down from a mountain, gouging out rock as it moves

GPS (global positioning system) receiver electronic gadget that detects signals from satellites in space and uses them to calculate its exact position on Earth's surface

hibernate go into a deep sleep during the winter to use as little energy as possible

indigenous people who originated in the place they now live

lava molten rock when it comes out of a volcano and flows across the surface. Lava turns to rock when it cools down.

magma molten rock under or in Earth's crust

mountain range collection of mountains in the same area of the world, such as the Himalayas or the Andes

nomad person who regularly moves from place to place instead of having a permanent home

off-piste away from prepared ski runs

pack animal animal that carries loads from place to place

pass gap or low point in a mountain range that people use to get from one side of the range to the other

pumice type of rock sometimes formed when a volcano erupts. It contains so many air bubbles that it floats.

pyroclastic flow roasting hot mixture of rock, ash, and gas that flows at high speed down the side of a volcano

ridge long, narrow mountain range

saddle lower part of a ridge between two higher points

species type of animal

summit highest part of a mountain. Some mountains have two or more high parts, which are all known as summits.

tectonic plate one of the giant pieces that form Earth's crust

tundra land in the Arctic that has soil that is always frozen under the surface

volcano place where magma from beneath Earth's crust comes out onto the surface, often building up a mountain

volcanologist person who studies volcanoes

FIND OUT MORE

Books

Explorers, Alasdair Macleod (Dorling Kindersley, 2010)

Horrible Geography: Freaky Peaks, Anita Ganeri (Scholastic, 2009)

Mountains (Habitat Survival), Melanie Waldron (Raintree, 2012)

Websites

www.bbc.co.uk/science/earth/natural_disasters/avalanche
This web page from the BBC has some amazing information and videos about avalanches.

www.evk2cnr.org/WebCams/PyramidOne/everest-webcam.html
This webcam shows live pictures of Mount Everest!

www.nhm.ac.uk/kids-only/earth-space/volcanoes/index.html
Find out more about volcanoes and different types of lava on the Natural History Museum's website.

www.theuiaa.org
The website of the International Mountaineering and Climbing Federation tells you everything you need to know about mountain climbing and expeditions, including information for young people.

volcanoes.usgs.gov
The volcano hazards section of the US Geological Survey site has links to webcams on some active volcanoes.

Places to visit

Geological Museum (part of the Natural History Museum)
Exhibition Road
South Kensington
London SW7 5BD
www.nhm.ac.uk

Arthur's seat, Edinburgh
This hill in the centre of Edinburgh is the remains of a volcano that erupted about 350 million years ago.

UK National Parks
Three of Britain's mountain ranges are National Parks that are open to visitors. They are the Lake District National Park, the Snowdonia National Park, and the Cairngorms National Park.

Cairngorm Mountain
www.cairngormmountain.org
A train can take you to the top of one of Britain's highest mountains.

Further research

Look back over the topics you have read about in the book. Which topics did you enjoy most – perhaps it was how mountains are made, or volcanoes, or mountain climbing, or mountain animals? Try researching your favourite topic in more detail, by visiting the websites listed here and others, and by visiting your local library.

INDEX